STUDY GUIDE

PURE|FLIX PRESENTS

GOD'S NOT DEAD

WHAT DO YOU BELIEVE?

BY RICE BROOCKS

God's Not Dead: What Do You Believe? Study Guide
© 2014 by Outreach, Inc.

All Scripture quotations marked *NIV* are taken from the Holy Bible, *New International Version* ®, NIV ®, Copyright ©1973, 1978, 1984, 2001 by Biblica. Used by permission of Zondervan Publishing House. All rights reserved worldwide.

All Scripture quotations marked *ESV* are from The Holy Bible, English Standard Version® (ESV®), copyright © 2001 by Crossway, a publishing ministry of Good News Publishers. Used by permission. All rights reserved.

ISBN: 9781970203164
Written by: Dr. Rice Broocks
Cover Design: Tim Downs
Interior Design: Stephanie Larson
Edited by: Julia Wallace
Printed in the United States of America

2 3 4 5 6 7 8 9 10

GOD'S NOT DEAD MOVIE STUDY GUIDE

TABLE OF CONTENTS

INTRODUCTION
#GODSNOTDEAD

"The reports of God's death have been greatly exaggerated."
—Willie Robertson of *Duck Dynasty*

The movie *God's Not Dead* has become a cultural phenomenon. Its success has been widely discussed, dissected, and debated. The movie did more than touch a nerve—it awakened Christians around the world to the reality that real faith isn't blind, which means the Christian faith is based on evidence. The focus of the movie is an introduction to the evidence that God indeed exists.

When a first year college student is challenged by his atheist professor to present his reasons for believing in God to his entire philosophy class, a drama unfolds that affects many lives, especially those listening to his classroom presentations.

Working with university students for more than thirty years prepared me to write the book *God's Not Dead*, which helped inspire the movie. It has been a great joy to watch people of all ages find a faith that is both reasonable and credible.

With the rise of skepticism concerning God's existence the past few decades, the need for believers to respond has never been greater. *God's Not Dead* the movie has helped spark a new generation to think about why they believe. God is alive and well in the twenty-first century.

Far from the predictions that faith in God would disappear, it is flourishing in places like Asia, Africa, Latin America and even Western nations like the US. This confounds the critics that assert that your faith is merely a product of where you're born.

The movie addresses this as you see people from a wide range of cultural experiences come to faith in God through their willingness to follow the evidence wherever it leads. That's because at the heart of this movie is a presentation of the evidence that God indeed exists. This defense of the faith is called apologetics. It comes from the Greek language, and means "defense or response." Apologetics is not apologizing for having faith or for mistakes done in the name of God, but making a logical case for God's existence and the credibility of the Christian faith. This is what the young hero of the film, Josh Wheaton (Shane Harper), is challenged to do.

One of the goals of the movie is to inspire millions of believers to be like Josh—to be able to give such a defense. By taking part in this study, you are becoming a part of that dream. This study guide is a "next step" for anyone serious about getting prepared to make such a defense of their faith. There are many valuable lessons the movie teaches in its various subplots—from the danger of shallow ungodly relationships to the empty pursuit of success apart from God. There's also a valuable lesson that demonstrates even those that appear closest to God in ministry can lose their faith and grow cynical.

The good news presented in the movie is that God's love and mercy extend to those close to Him as well as those that are farthest away (Ephesians 2:17).

While there are many themes that could be discussed in this study guide, the focus is on the classroom scenes that consisted of the key arguments in Josh's defense of the belief in God's existence. The movie touched on three key pieces of evidence:

1. **The beginning of the Universe**
2. **The origin of life**
3. **Evil and suffering**

While both the Scripture and the gospel are mentioned in the movie, the focus is on these foundational truths.

Hebrews 11:6 says, *"Without faith it is impossible to please God, because anyone who comes to him must believe that he exists and that he rewards those who earnestly seek him"* (NIV). That's why we say that belief in God is the "ground zero" of faith. If you don't believe in God, then you won't believe He could have inspired the Bible to be written or sent His Son to die for the sins of the world.

By mastering the fundamentals presented in the movie and explained in greater detail in the book *God's Not Dead*, you should be able to not only survive the assault of skepticism, but thrive in any setting regardless of the challenge.

The movie, therefore, was ultimately designed to give believers confidence—confidence in God and in the gospel of His Son Jesus Christ.

When discussing the evidence for God, which can sometimes include technical explanations involving philosophy, science, and history; I constantly tell my teenage sons, "This might be a little over your head, but it's not out of your reach."

Let's shake off the intellectual laziness and spiritual apathy and do the hard work that real faith requires. In the end, you will be able to confidently proclaim to anyone in any setting: God's not dead.

GET PREPARED

KEY VERSE:
"But in your hearts set apart Christ as Lord. Always be prepared to give an answer to everyone who asks you to give the reason for the hope that you have. But do this with gentleness and respect." —1 Peter 3:15, NIV

KEY MOVIE QUOTE:
"Mr. Wheaton, are you ready?" —Professor Radisson to Josh Wheaton

KEY MOVIE SCENE:
Lesson one - Clip 1

OPENING DISCUSSION QUESTIONS
1. Discuss the overall impact the movie had on you.
2. Were you able to invite friends to view it that were not Christians? What was their response?
3. Has the movie inspired you to be able to defend your faith?

INTRODUCTION TO THE LESSON
The theme of this first lesson is to be prepared to defend your faith. Our key verse says "always be prepared." From the very beginning of your walk with Christ there have been opportunities and challenges to the commitment you've made.

In the past few years, there has been a disturbing trend of young people letting go of their faith once they leave high school and go to college. This trend is not due to the lack of credibility of the Christian faith, but the fact that most don't know the reasons they believe.

You must have more than a subjective experience to survive the onslaught of unbelief that the culture around you will present. This challenge happened to me during my third year at college when I surrendered my life to Christ. I was immediately challenged by my atheist brother who was in his final year of law school. He despised Christianity and made it his personal mission to talk me out of my faith. I'm so grateful that people around me, both pastors and friends, taught me the basic truths that we will study in this lesson. As my brother started his speech on why my faith was not true, I had a response. He actually began to doubt his doubts because of the simple truths I spoke to him. On the weekend he intended to talk me out of my faith, he was baptized.

This study can be an important step in not only helping you build a faith that can stand the tests and trials that await, but giving you confidence to help others as well.

PRINCIPLES OF PREPARATION

1. Be committed.
"But in your hearts revere Christ as Lord. Always be prepared to give an answer to everyone who asks you to give the reason for the hope that you have. But do this with gentleness and respect." —1 Peter 3:15, NIV

Without question, the most important part of your witness is your own commitment to Christ. When the Scripture tells us to "always be prepared," it first says to "sanctify [set apart] Christ as Lord in your hearts." For Jesus to be Lord means that we completely submit to Him. Many assume that simply saying they believe is enough.

Jesus said:
"Why do you call me Lord, Lord and do not do what I say?"
—Luke 6:46, NIV

When your heart is devoted to Him, then it's a matter of discerning His will for you and His instructions for your life and not just following our feelings or our friends' opinions.

When Josh was challenged to sign the paper declaring, "God is dead," his commitment to be a Christian meant that his decision was already made. When his girlfriend tried to convince him to go ahead and "sign the stupid paper," he was tested to follow Christ or compromise his beliefs due to pressure.

The word Lord means God. Practically, it means that He is in charge of our lives—He's the boss! When we call ourselves Christians and don't obey His word, we are in danger of living hypocritical lives and becoming a stumbling block to others. One of the excuses people use who have rejected God are the failures of those that claim to believe.

Basically, this means we need to be willing to stand up and be identified as a believer, regardless of the consequences. A verse that gets repeated in the movie is Matthew 10:32–33.

Jesus said, *"Whoever acknowledges Me before others, I will also acknowledge before My father in heaven. But whoever disowns Me before others, I will disown before My father in heaven"* (NIV).

Josh's decision to publicly defend his belief in God was motivated by this truth. It was also the motivation of *Duck Dynasty* stars Willie and Korrie Robertson.

For Mina, Professor Radisson's girlfriend, the verse that challenged her was 2 Corinthians 6:14 (to not be "unequally yoked" with unbelievers). Again, this is where Scripture is clear about how we are to live our lives; we are called to obey God and not our feelings.

When we do this we show that we are not merely giving lip service to our faith, but we are sincere Christians.

2. Be ready.
"And with your feet fitted with the readiness that comes from the gospel of peace." —Ephesians 6:15, NIV

We should always be ready to give the reasons for our hope. This study will cover some of the reasons that we should be able to give to others. Of course, our own testimony of God's work in our lives is always effective. We can get ready by preparing to give a concise two-minute personal testimony: an overview of what we were like before we knew God, what happened to change our lives, and what our lives are like as a result of Christ working in our hearts.

Many times people need to have questions answered that are hindering their ability to believe in God. With a little effort to study and prepare, we can help others find a true and fulfilling faith. Josh didn't start preparing when his professor challenged him on the first day of class. He had been reading and studying since he was in junior high school (remember he met his girlfriend at a Christian concert six years before). He also referenced his high-school yearbook quote from the legendary Christian writer C. S. Lewis, "Only a real risk can test the quality of a belief." The actor who played Josh, Shane Harper, told me during the filming of the movie that he had loved studying apologetics and learning to defend his faith to skeptics and unbelievers. This preparation helped Shane be ready when the opportunity was presented for him to be in the movie *God's Not Dead*.

We get ready by learning the reasons to believe. The evidence is all around us (through the world God made, and within us—speaking of the complexity of living things). Beyond these things, we all possess a sense of morality. As you master these truths, you will be able to give the basic evidence that points to the reality of God's existence.

Atheists try to paint the picture that you must choose between faith and reason. Yet real faith is reasonable. At the same time, all reason contains faith. Everyone's reason is based on things that must be assumed. We all look at the world with a set of assumptions that are called our *worldview*. If you think that there can be nothing beyond nature you have the *worldview* called *naturalism*. But if you believe that nature can't explain it all, then you have a view of the world that makes room for the existence of a supernatural creator.

Being ready obviously means you need to have a basic understanding of the Bible and the Christian faith as a whole. You should regularly read the Scriptures with commentaries that will explain the background and context of the books in the Bible you are studying. The greater your understanding of these things, the more easily you can explain Christian truths to others.

3. Be wise.
"The one who is wise saves lives." —Proverbs 11:30, NIV

After Josh was challenged by his professor to publicly defend his faith, he did not act recklessly or arrogantly. He respectfully negotiated with the teacher to have the class decide whether his defense of his faith was credible. This was indeed a wise decision. This highlights one of the most important aspects that should guide our lives: godly wisdom.

On almost a daily basis for most of my Christian life, reading a chapter in the book of Proverbs has been a routine. The constant theme is that God's wisdom is available for those that seek it. Wisdom is described as being more valuable than silver and gold. Undoubtedly we have all seen and heard people who are filled with excitement about the Lord, but who possess very little wisdom. This leads them to do many foolish and embarrassing things. I can certainly remember doing those kinds of things as a new believer. I'm so grateful that God offers to give wisdom to anyone who asks. This wisdom will lead us to speak the right words at the right time in order to maximize the impact of our words.

You can learn to choose the best times and places to speak about your faith. You should learn from more experienced Christians about how to be the best witness for Christ in the different areas of your life. The greater your insight, the more readily God can use you in different settings.

Notice when weighing whether he should follow through with his public defense of his faith, Josh went to the church to pray and seek God's guidance. He displayed wisdom by listening to the counsel of Dave, the campus pastor, who spoke to him about the importance of his witness to the students in the class who might never go to church. Pastor Dave offered him two verses of Scripture to ponder before making his final decision. In the end, Josh allowed the Scripture to guide him instead of his feelings or fears.

This wisdom comes through Scripture, our parents, godly leaders, friends, and of course through prayer. God can give us supernatural insight on when to speak, what questions to ask, and what to say as we ask him for wisdom (James 1:5).

In the end, like Josh, we can find ourselves in situations that seem overwhelming and beyond our ability to succeed. God's wisdom can guide us through these seemingly impossible situations and bring about almost miraculous results.

4. Be humble.
"Humble yourselves, therefore, under God's mighty hand, that he may lift you up in due time." — 1 Peter 5:6, NIV

At the end of Josh's first classroom presentation, Professor Radisson asked him a question Josh could not answer. He was not defensive about his ignorance, but he simply said, "I don't know." Likewise, we should not pretend that we have all of the answers to everyone's questions. We can never fully address all the issues with which Christians have struggled for hundreds of years. We also should not present ourselves as intellectually or morally superior to those to whom we are talking. Instead, we are bearing witness to the God who showed us His mercy. And, we are sharing the reasons we have learned that our faith is based on solid reason and evidence.

The challenge Josh faced to defend his faith in front of an entire class will probably not happen to you. Instead, you will enter into spiritual discussions with friends or people you randomly meet who have doubts or questions about the truth of the Christian faith. In such situations, learning to ask questions and listen to others is as important as having good answers! Some will become more open to the gospel simply because you showed them respect and honestly listened to them.

At times, people will become angry when hearing anything said about God. They may even respond with insults and ridicule. It is vital that we don't take this personally, but seek to understand the real cause of their opposition. Their comments could stem from past bad experiences or misunderstandings. Often, our kindness will diffuse much of this immediate opposition to Christianity, which comes from more emotional reasons than intellectual. You can ask more questions about the reasons for their anger and how they arrived at their beliefs. This information will guide you in knowing how to best speak to them.

The key verse in this lesson says that we are to always be prepared to give the reason for the hope of our faith and do it with "gentleness and respect." This will be difficult to do without the help of the Holy Spirit. It is helpful for me to remember how patient God has been with me in spite of my own failings. When we remain mindful of how kind and gentle the Lord has been with us, it will keep our hearts right as we deal with skeptics and their opposition.

God honors our efforts to share about Him, regardless of our effectiveness or how many times we fall short. As we faithfully continue to reach out, He will give us insight on when to speak and what to say. We need to constantly pray for His guidance and wisdom. As long as we remain dependent on Him to empower us, our words can impact those around us.

5. Be confident.

"The wicked flee though no one persues, but the righteous are bold as a lion." —Proverbs 28:1, NIV

We can be both humble and confident at the same time. This is because the evidence for the truth of our faith is both extensive and compelling. As we will discuss in this study, there is powerful evidence for God that comes from science, history, and philosophy. Skeptics often argue that they can see no evidence for God in spite of what seems to be obvious and plain to those who believe. They only see the evidence that fits their stories, the rest is ignored or suppressed (Romans 1:20). In reality, they don't doubt Christianity because the evidence points them away from its reality, but because they have made a choice from the start to reject it. Therefore they interpret the evidence through the filter that God does not exist. Knowing this should give us confidence to speak even if they don't agree with what we are saying.

We can be confident because the Holy Spirit has been given to help us as we share with others. This reality can't be stressed enough. Jesus said, *"You will receive power when the Holy Spirit comes on you and you; will be my witnesses"* (Acts 1:8, NIV). Over the years, I have been in countless situations where I've talked with people more educated than me and with far more intellectual ability. Yet the Holy Spirit has given me wisdom and knowledge that is truly remarkable. One word from God can change people forever. Even the Apostle Paul asked that people pray for him to boldly proclaim the gospel. (Ephesians 6:19). As we are filled with the power of the Spirit, extraordinary things can happen.

Finally, we can be confident because of the change that God has produced in our lives. In one of the most famous encounters with Jesus, a man who had been healed said, "I was blind and now I see." In the end, your personal testimony of God's mercy and grace is more than enough to give you the motivation to fearlessly tell others about Him. Once on campus at the University of California Berkley, we were conducting an outdoor campus meeting that drew the ire of many skeptics. It seemed the evidence I was giving about the Lord was being completely ignored. When all seemed lost, a student came to the front of the crowd and began to give her testimony. All of the anger and resistance seemed to drain out of those in attendance. This young girl's story of God's working in her life could not be refuted. Her boldness was an inspiration to me then, and still motivates me today. It reminds me that we can stand in front of anyone and testify about the reality of God's existence because of what He's done for us.

CONCLUSION

The first thing we must do in our preparation to defend the faith is to submit our lives completely to Christ as Lord. In doing this we allow His Word to direct our decisions as well as remove the things that He says are sins.

God will honor our efforts as we prepare to be faithful witnesses for Him. As a result we will find God directing people our way who are searching for Him. It's important to not make the mistake of thinking you have to have all the answers. While we must be prepared, we should also not be afraid to simply say that we don't know when we're faced with questions that are beyond our abilities to handle. However, this should motivate us to keep learning when we encounter these types of situations. We should be in a state of constant preparation.

This will result in a deep confidence in the reality of our faith and the power of God's Spirit to lead us regardless of what circumstances or challenges we face. Like Josh, though the odds seem stacked against us, we can truly be more than conquerors.

CLOSING DISCUSSION QUESTIONS
1) Do you feel you have surrendered all to Christ as Lord?
2) Are you challenged to study and learn to defend your faith?
3) Are there people challenging you now to prove that God is real or that Christianity is true?

AS A GROUP
Before your group ends its time together, allow a few minutes for everyone to write his or her two-minute personal testimony. Think of it as an overview of what you were like before you knew God, what happened to change your life, what your life is like as a result of Christ working in your heart, and how God is teaching and using you.

Next, have each person practice sharing his or her brief testimony with a partner or in front of the whole group. If you are using this study on your own, find a friend or family member you can tell your testimony to.

A MOMENT OF YOUR OWN
Consider your own questions and confidence when it comes to standing for or explaining what you believe:

1. What has held me back from proclaiming or defending my faith in Christ?
2. What motivates me to dig deeper into a better understanding of the reasoning behind my faith?
3. What are the areas that I want and need to study and prepare further?

FOLLOW UP

Read one chapter of Proverbs each morning this week. Chose one verse to re-read and focus on throughout the day.

Read Ephesians 6:15. How does it fit within Ephesians 6:10-17?

Choose one step you can take to prepare yourself to be ready to stand firm in the Gospel.

Read and meditate on 1 Peter 3:15. List one way each that you can demonstrate boldness, gentleness and respect to people who do not believe in God.

*Additional reading from *God's Not Dead: Evidence for God in an Age of Uncertainty:*
- Introduction – Ground Zero of Faith
- Chapter 1 – God's Not Dead

LESSON TWO

HAVE
NO
FEAR

KEY VERSE

"Blessed are you when people insult you, persecute you and falsely say all kinds of evil against you because of me. Rejoice and be glad, because great is your reward in heaven, for in the same way they persecuted the prophets who were before you." —Matthew 5:11-12, NIV

KEY MOVIE QUOTE

"There's only room in this relationship for two.... No room for a dead carpenter turned itinerant Rabbi."

KEY SCENES

Lesson two - Clip 1

Clip 2

Clip 3

OPENING DISCUSSION QUESTIONS

1. Do these scenarios seem realistic to you?
2. Have you ever faced persecution for your faith?
3. What do you think about the characters' responses to the persecutions faced?

INTRODUCTION OF THE LESSON

One of the major themes of the movie is the persecution people face because of their faith. Some have suggested that this is overstated and that our world is far more tolerant today. The facts suggest otherwise. In many countries of the world, to profess faith in Christ is to lose freedom. Every year, literally thousands of people around the world lose their lives because they are Christians.

In America, a nation where tolerance has become a cultural commandment, intolerance for those who believe in the Christian worldview and biblical morality can be grossly unfair and, at times, absurd. This has resulted in believers feeling intimidated. The attitude is that if you keep your faith private, everything will be ok. Professor Radisson responded to Josh's statement about being a Christian, "You can always go home and sink to your knees and pray at your bedside … but what you do in this class is my business." Another challenge is moral relativism. This is the philosophy that all beliefs are equally right. While people certainly have the freedom to believe what they want to believe (God is the one that grants all people that choice), that doesn't mean that all beliefs are true.

I once met a woman on an airplane who told me she was God. I told her, "If you're God, I've got a lot of questions for you." Obviously the woman's beliefs were not true. However, most of the time deception is much more subtle.

As believers, God calls us to a very simple walk of faith and obedience. As Pastor Dave said to Josh, *"It's simple, but not easy."* As followers of Christ, we have submitted our lives to Him and His Word. Regardless of our feelings or our friends' opinions, we ultimately listen to Christ. Like Jesus, our attitude should be "not my will, but thine be done."

When we decide to follow Christ, we can come into direct conflict with those who say they believe in God but have no desire to obey His Word.

As Jesus told His disciples, *"Trouble or persecution comes because of the Word."* —Mark 44:17, NIV

Many have wondered whether the persecution in the movie was realistic. Dr. Ming Wang, a respected eye surgeon who came to study at Harvard University from China, told me that the persecution the Chinese student (Martin) experienced from his father was very realistic. Ming was an atheist when he came to Harvard, but he became a Christian based on the testimony of a professor. His story was actually an inspiration for the student in the movie.

PRINCIPLES OF LESSON

1. Don't be surprised.
"Dear friends, do not be surprised at the fiery ordeal that has come on you to test you, as though something strange were happening to you.

But rejoice inasmuch as you participate in the sufferings of Christ, so that you may be overjoyed when his glory is revealed. If you are insulted because of the name of Christ, you are blessed, for the Spirit of glory and of God rests on you." —1 Peter 4:12–14, NIV

From the day I became a follower of Christ, I knew that my new life and commitment wasn't going to make everyone happy. My parents didn't really understand what was happening to me. They could see I was happier and that made them happy, but they could also see that I was reading my Bible and not going to the same places and parties I usually frequented. Some of my friends called me and said they were concerned for me. Those closest to me thought I was going too far in this religious thing.

In the movie, you see this happening in almost all of those that are seeking to follow Jesus. Josh faces it from his girlfriend and his parents when he tries to take his faith public (he mentions that his parents don't want him risking a bad grade in class should he choose to accept the professor's challenge). Martin, the student from China, is surprised that his father is so negative when he brings up the subject of God instead of focusing on his schoolwork. Ayisha, the young girl, certainly faces painful persecution from her Muslim father when it comes to light that she believes in Jesus Christ. In fact, her father challenges her to say, "There is one God, he is not begotten." This is his attempt to get her to renounce her faith that Jesus is the "only begotten Son" of God (John 3:16). Mina, Professor Radisson's girlfriend, feels his scorn when she mentions that she's a Christian.

Obviously, this is not always the case. Most people will say nothing to you and they will treat you fairly when they find out you are a believer. Remember, 95 percent of the people in the United States say they believe in God. As we mentioned, while many say they believe, they are moral relativists and don't attempt to live by God's Word or His standard described in Scripture. Josh's girlfriend is the perfect example of this mindset. Though she would have considered herself as much as a believer as Josh, she didn't feel her faith should get in the way of career plans or opportunities. She actually scoffed at the notion that he wanted to put God first even over her wishes.

By no means should we have a "persecution complex." All of our troubles won't be because people don't like our faith. We simply are told to not be surprised when it does happen. We must be prepared to respond to others graciously and with kindness.

2. Don't be afraid.
"Do not fear their threats; do not be frightened." —1 Peter 3:14, NIV

Over and over again we are told in the Bible to not be afraid. Nothing can be more important to remember when it comes to standing up for your faith. For us to share our faith with others, we must first ensure that we ourselves are free from this kind of paralyzing fear. For instance, if we fear criticism, we learn that we still feel our identity and value is based on the opinions of others instead of God's acceptance. Likewise, if we fear the consequences of telling others about Christ, we learn that we trust in our circumstances and the decisions of others more than on Jesus' promise to take care of us (Matthew 6:25–34). Or, if we fear not obtaining some desire or goal, we learn that we have placed our hope for meaning and fulfillment in some worldly achievement over the incalculable value of being part of God's kingdom. As these fears come to the surface, we can share them with fellow believers and pray for God's power to break us free from the grip of this kind of stronghold (2 Corinthians 10:4). Once we have become truly free of the fear we become mighty instruments in God's hands.

One of the things we are told to do to overcome fear is to meditate on God's promises. As a young believer, I learned this wonderful verse, *"For the Spirit God gave us does not make us timid, but gives us power, love and self-discipline"* (2 Timothy 1:7, NIV). Over and over this promise brought me comfort and peace when fear would try to overwhelm me.

I also learned the same verse that Pastor Dave told Ayisha when she came to his office for counsel. *"I can do all this through him who gives me strength"* (Philippians 4:13, NIV). As we meditate and then speak the promises, fear will lose its grip over us. It's good to make a list of the promises in God's Word that promises us freedom from fear. It's been said that we are told more than 365 times to "fear not" or "don't be afraid." That should tell us that God wants us to be free from fear on a daily basis.

Finally, even if we feel fear it should not stop us from moving forward and doing the right thing. Many times the feeling of intimidation leaves when you face it and refuse to back down.

3. Don't React.

"Do not repay evil with evil or insult with insult." —1 Peter 3:9, NIV

There are many reasons why someone may be reacting to you in an adversarial way because of your faith in God. You must try and keep this in mind so that you don't respond to them in anger. In fact, the Scripture says that unbelievers are blinded by "the god of this world" that is Satan (2 Corinthians 4:4). This should give us compassion and patience to keep in mind that this is indeed a spiritual battle. Like Professor Radisson in the movie, their hostility might be the result of painful experiences in the past. In the professor's case, it was losing his mother to cancer after asking God to heal her. As we will study in week five, pain and suffering is a huge stumbling block for many people when it comes to believing that God is loving and kind. That is why one of the first things I try to do is find out the source of that pain. Josh does that when he asks Professor Radisson, "What happened to you?"

Others may be reacting to you because they may feel that Christians are narrow minded and bigoted. Again, they fail to realize that in fact they have become just that by prejudging you. Whatever the case, our ability to not respond to their insults with insults can go a long way toward dismantling these false notions. In philosophy this is called *a straw-man argument*—this means people build a false picture of something or someone and then they attack it. Many times I have had to dismantle the false notions of what Christians believe and what others have done in the name of Christ. When someone says that all Christians are hypocrites, I help them realize that it isn't fair to label almost two billion people because of the actions of a few that have hurt them or disillusioned them.

Remember, *insults aren't arguments*. You must not focus on the insults that others are speaking against you, but keep the focus on the truth and reasonableness of your beliefs. In doesn't matter how many bad things people who claim to believe in God have done, God still exists. I have five children; just because my children may do something wrong doesn't mean I don't exist.

Eventually, the force of truth will cause even the hardest heart to soften. Indeed that's why the angry atheist professor who persecuted believers accepts Christ in the end.

4. Don't stop sharing.
"We cannot help speaking about what we have seen and heard."
—Acts 4:20, NIV

The Bible tells us that there is an enemy to mankind whose name is Satan. Far from a character in a red suit with horns and a pitch fork, he is an evil entity that indeed exists. The Apostle Paul tells us that we are literally wrestling with principalities, powers, and evil spirits that are affecting hearts and minds (Ephesians 6:10). It would be safe to say that a clear goal of that enemy was to shut down the preaching of the gospel and the truth that God exists. That's why it is vital that you don't allow persecution to shut down your witness. Regardless of how painful things may be, you must persevere. This is what the Scripture is speaking about in Acts 4:29. The apostles were arrested and warned to stop telling the gospel to others. They responded, *"We cannot help speaking about what we have seen and heard."* The persecution in the early Church was severe. The Roman emperors hated the followers of Christ because they proclaimed He was a King. In fact, they said that every knee would bow to Jesus (Philippians 2:10-11). That was indeed threatening to them. As believers, we answer to God and He calls us to live in light of His authority. Yes, we are to be respectful of earthly authorities. We do all that we can to live godly lives and be respectful, but that doesn't mean we stop sharing our faith.

I recently spoke with a science professor at a university in the United States. He had taught a class called the Boundaries of Science where he simply showed that science demonstrates that the universe, as well as life itself, had the markings of design. He came under severe scrutiny due to a concerted campaign from atheist groups who wanted to stop his voice. Though the university eventually cancelled his class, he did not stop speaking. He continues to take his message to campus groups, churches, and anyone else who will listen. Far from defeated, he knows he must continue to speak the truth.

Like this professor, you might have to alter your strategy, but you don't have to stop sharing. Sometimes what seems to be a door closing could actually mean the opening of an even wider door for your witness. God will give you wisdom through His Word and through the counsel of godly friends and leaders. In the end, God's Word will not return empty (Isaiah 55:11).

5. Don't give up.

"Be alert and of sober mind. Your enemy the devil prowls around like a roaring lion looking for someone to devour. Resist him, standing firm in the faith, because you know that the family of believers throughout the world is undergoing the same kind of sufferings. And the God of all grace, who called you to his eternal glory in Christ, after you have suffered a little while, will himself restore you and make you strong, firm and steadfast." —1 Peter 5:8–10, NIV

Often, the cares and worries of this world can distract us from God's purposes for our lives. In particular, we can lose focus on our mission to share the gospel. Becoming more vocal about your faith can make you feel alone and vulnerable. *Don't give up!* The negative reactions can take their toll on your own self-image and sense of worth. However, if we are motivated by God's love and guided by the Holy Spirit, our efforts will eventually bear fruit. Often, people will recognize you as a genuine Christian, and they will come to you for spiritual counsel and guidance. Even some who initially show the most hostility may eventually ask you to explain your beliefs. Few today demonstrate great conviction for anything of substance, so just your passion for God will make you a light in the darkness and a beacon of hope.

In challenging environments we may feel at times that no one has any interest in paying any heed to your witness. *Don't give up!* Be assured that even if your faithfulness does not result in immediate results, it will definitely shape your character and faith. God will be working in you to prepare you for future opportunities. Also, be encouraged that the seeds you sow now could grow over a period of years, eventually resulting in a person coming to know Christ years in the future. Finally, know that the angels in heaven are rejoicing over your faithful witness, which is part of your worship to God.

As an even greater challenge, you may be in settings where the hostility toward you as a Christian is unyielding and seemingly unbearable. Like Ayisha, who was kicked out of her home for believing in Jesus, you might feel like you can't continue. *Don't give up!* Your righteous life will shine a light onto the lifestyles of those in rebellion to God and expose in their hearts their rebellion. Instead of allowing that conviction to bring them to repentance, they will suppress the truth and instead lash out in anger toward you. Their immediate attacks against you could be challenging, but the light of truth may eventually lead them to Christ.

CONCLUSION

Today, there is more persecution against Christians than any time in history. That seems strange in a world where we imagine technology and globilization should have brought more tolerance and understanding to everyone. Yet, the dynamic and piercing claims of Christ have set Him apart from anyone else who has ever lived. He indeed is Lord of all.

One of the promises of God that no one claims is found in 2 Timothy 3:12, *"Everyone who wants to live a godly life in Christ Jesus will be persecuted"* (NIV). May we all rise up and shake off fear and intimidation and boldly proclaim our faith to a dark and hurting world.

CLOSING DISCUSSION QUESTIONS
1. Have you ever been persecuted for being a Christian or for sharing about your faith?
2. Is fear a hindrance for you when it comes to deciding whether you should share with others?
3. Which part of this particular lesson has encouraged you the most?

AS A GROUP

With partners or in small groups, role-play to practice facing the following scenarios.

1. A friend tells you, "Lighten up. Quit taking this God stuff so seriously."
2. An acquaintance or stranger insults you and says, "Christians are ignorant hypocrites. I can't believe you actually believe those Bible fairy tales!"
3. A teacher or boss tells you, "Please refrain from religious discussions. It doesn't belong in the office or classroom."

A MOMENT OF YOUR OWN

Jesus didn't run from suffering. His disciples also learned to rely on the Holy Spirit's strength to stand boldly in the face of persecution. Complete the following prayers as openly and honestly as you can. Repeat this prayer exercise daily through the coming week.

Father, you have called me to be your child and a co-heir with Christ (Romans 8:17). I want to share in His glory. Please forgive me for trying to avoid sharing in His suffering by

_____

_____

Jesus, thank you that you have promised your comfort in the face of suffering (2 Corinthians 1:7). Your faithfulness is unfailing. Thank you for meeting my needs when

_____

_____

Jesus, you suffered deeply and willingly for me. Please help me to respond with gratitude and grace by

_____

_____

Please fill me with your strength to find joy in you—even in the face of persecution and problems. Fill me with your boldness and enable me to

_____

_____

FOLLOW UP

Meditate on God's promises. Make a list of Bible verses that fill you with freedom from fear.

Read and reflect on 1 Peter 4:12-16. List one to three ways you can rejoice in persecution or suffering through Christ's strength.

Read 2 Timothy 1:7. Make a list of your fears related to sharing or defending your faith. One at a time, cross out your fear and replace it with a phrase of hope that you want to see God do.

*Additional reading from *God's Not Dead: Evidence for God in an Age of Uncertainty:*
- Chapter 2 – Real Faith Isn't Blind

EMBRACE THE EVIDENCE

KEY VERSE

"In the beginning God created the heavens and the earth."
—Genesis 1:1, NIV

KEY MOVIE QUOTE

"Belgian astronomer George Lemaitre ... said that the entire universe jumping into existence in a trillionth of the trillionth of a second out of nothingness in an unimaginably intense flash of light is how he would expect the universe to respond if God were to actually utter the command in Genesis 1:3, 'Let there be light.'"

KEY SCENE

Lesson three - Clip 1
            Clip 2

OPENING DISCUSSION QUESTIONS

1. What did you think about how Josh started by saying they were "putting God on trial"?
2. Were you nervous watching him as he spoke (wondering how good he would be)?
3. If this happened in real life, do you think other classmates would have had the courage to not sign the paper?

INTRODUCTION TO LESSON

Josh begins his public defense by stating that God is on trial. This phrase was taken from the essays of C. S. Lewis who spoke of "God in the dock." The *dock* was the term for the witness stand in England where an accused person stands on trial. Of course, Jesus was put on trial two thousand years ago, and though He was innocent, he was condemned in order to satisfy the desires of His enemies.

Josh begins his argument by showing that creation itself points to the reality of a Creator. Science is the natural place to start his defense, since the evidence for God in the very order of the universe is beyond reasonable doubt. Skeptics fail to appreciate this argument because they often demand to see direct physical evidence. However, we would not expect to find physical evidence for God in creation any more than we would expect to find physical evidence of Steven Jobs by looking inside an iPhone. Instead, we would see in the iPhone's design a clear picture of the creativity and genius of its designer. The same holds true for the design behind the laws and properties of nature. As Paul stated to the church in Rome, *"God's invisible qualities—his eternal power and divine nature—have been clearly seen."* —Romans 1:20, NIV

PRINCIPLES OF LESSON

1. The evidence is clearly seen.

Josh starts his defense of the existence of God at the most logical place—the beginning. He states, "Most cosmologists now agree that the universe began some 13.7 billion years ago." As a short digression, many Christians believe the universe and the earth are much younger than the age held by most mainstream scientists—thousands of years instead of billions. A critical point to recognize is that Christians should not get caught up in debates about secondary issues, such as the age of the earth, especially when brilliant Christian scholars hold differing opinions. Josh's point is not to debate the age of the universe, but to bring up the dramatic evidence that the universe had a beginning, which means there must be an initial or uncaused cause that began everything.

The fact of a beginning directly disproves the common belief held by scientists from Aristotle to Einstein that the universe was eternal; that is, it had no beginning or end. The evidence for a beginning became undeniable with the discoveries in physics and astronomy in the early twentieth century, which led to the theory called the "Big Bang." This phrase was originally a derogatory term coined by those who recognized that saying the universe had a beginning, allows "a divine foot in the door." Namely, it suggests a "beginner" or creator of everything. The logic of this could be stated in three simple statements:
1. Everything that begins to exist has a cause.
2. The universe began to exist.
3. Therefore, the universe has a cause.

The amazing thing is that when the universe began, space and time began as well. One of the foremost Christian philosophers and apologists is Dr. William Lane Craig. He points out the in light of this logic, the cause of the universe must be infinite, timeless, uncaused, and eternal. This is the beginning of a definition for God who is also rational, moral, and personal. All of these properties that exist in the universe; therefore, must be possessed by the Creator as well.

Scientists, especially physicists, have long recognized that the laws of nature seem to have been carefully designed with human life in mind. The universe appears to be fine-tuned for life.[1] For instance, if the force of gravity were only slightly larger or smaller, no planets would exist. These and other scientific discoveries have made even many atheistic physicists acknowledge that science points to an intelligent designer. As Fred Hoyle, a famous astronomer stated, "A common sense interpretation of the facts suggests that a superintellect has monkeyed with physics, as well as with chemistry and biology, and that there are no blind forces worth speaking about in nature."[2] Even committed skeptics begrudgingly concede these facts.

2. The evidence is pervasive.
Moreover, the evidence for God extends well beyond physics into virtually every branch of science. For instance, countless features of our planet had to be perfectly crafted for it to support complex life. The following are just a few examples of the many details that had to be carefully set:
- distance of the earth from sun
- the earth's rotation rate and length of a year
- amount of water on the Earth's surface
- types and amount of gasses in Earth's atmosphere
- size of the moon and its distance from the Earth
- location of the Earth within our galaxy

Physicists have identified hundreds of other examples that are related

1. For several specific examples, see www.reasons.org.
2. Fred Hoyle, "The Universe: Past and Present Reflection," *Annual Reviews of Astronomy and Astrophysics;* 20 (1982): 16.

to the design of our sun, our moon, life, and even our galaxy. Some of the examples even connect different fields of science. For instance, the properties of light leaving our sun are perfect for photosynthesis in plants, an important process in biology. These same properties allow the lenses in our eyes to create highly focused and detailed images, an important property in eyesight. Scores of other examples were collected by the physicist Hugh Ross on his website.[3] You should memorize at least a few that you can easily explain.

The chance of so many details being so perfectly set is unimaginably small, even given the number of planets in our universe. As an illustration of the implications, imagine a hiker coming across a cabin in the woods. Inside the cabin, the hiker found her favorite food in the refrigerator, her favorite movies on the mantle next to the TV, pictures of her relatives on the shelf, and a cell phone with numbers programmed in for her best friends in order of preference. The hiker would naturally assume that all of those details were not coincidences; someone knew she was coming. Similarly, the details in nature were perfectly set for the existence of intelligent life. This fact indicates that our Creator designed our universe and planet with us in mind.

Equally striking, the same factors that allow us to live on earth, also allow us to advance culturally and scientifically. For instance, the atmosphere not only has the right gases for us to breath, it is also transparent, so we can study the stars. Also, the amount of oxygen in air is sufficiently high for us to easily produce fire, so our ancestors could create metal tools. However, the amount is not so high that fires spread uncontrollably and destroy most of the forests. All of these examples show that our planet was specifically designed not just for life in general, but particularly for mankind.

3. The evidence is suppressed.
Many skeptics suppress the natural conclusion of design by appealing to a number of excuses. This is what the Apostle Paul is referring to when he states that people "suppress the truth" (Romans 1:18). Some have claimed that the universe could have

3. www.reasons.org

created itself. Others propose the existence of fantastically large numbers of other universes. However, none of these proposals are based on even the slightest amount of evidence. In other words, skeptics' denial of a Creator is based purely on blind faith.

Some have been very open in saying that they would accept any explanation, no matter how unlikely, in order to avoid belief in God. Another common tactic has been to ignore the evidence and simply assert that science and faith are inherently in conflict. This claim is the exact opposite of the truth. Modern science was, in fact, largely developed by Christians who studied nature because of their faith. They expected it to be governed by orderly laws because it was created by an orderly law giver. Moreover, they believed that we could discover and comprehend that order because we were crafted in the Creator's image. Other skeptics, such as Richard Dawkins, argue that a person cannot claim that God created the universe without addressing the questions of who created God. That kind of thinking leads to absurdity. Dawkins is saying that we must have an explanation for our explanation in order to offer it as plausible. Here's a simple way to look at it: If you're walking through the woods and you see a turtle on a fencepost, you wouldn't have to know how it got there to come to the logical conclusion that it didn't get there on its own. In the same way there is no way the universe can be its own cause.

4. The evidence is supernatural.

The cumulative evidence does not simply point to a generic designer, but it reveals many of His specific characteristics. For instance, physicists have recognized that time and space itself seemed to have come into existence at the creation event. Therefore, the creator had to exist outside of time and space. In addition, since every detail of nature was designed for His purposes, we know that the creator is unimaginably powerful. And, since the creator specifically shaped every detail of earth for the benefit of people, we can tell He is personal, directly involved in our world, and caring. In summary, the facts show that the creator is all-powerful, timeless, personal, involved, and caring, all of which points quite clearly to the God of the Bible.

Skeptics often deny before even examining the evidence the possibility of God being involved in our world. They say that appealing to miracles undermines the very discipline of science. However, miracles do not represent the denial or breaking of the laws of nature. Because we know consistent laws exist, we can know when something extraordinary has happened. Miracles are simply places where God acts in ways that are atypical and special. Ironically, while atheists deny the possibility of miracles, they require many of their own in order to explain the universe as well as life coming into existence out of absolutely nothing. As Josh says in this first classroom defense, "In real life we don't see things jumping into existence out of nothingness. Atheists want to make one small exception, the universe and everything in it."

There is no question that life is filled with the evidence of design. As an example, a geologist discovering Mt. Rushmore would not be abandoning geology by recognizing that the images of the presidents were created by an intelligent being. Because of his knowledge, he recognizes that the nature of the faces is very different from what natural forces would produce. For instance, they are much smoother and more regular. He would simply recognize that in this particular instance, some intelligence has acted to create a majestic work of art. Likewise, the authors of the Bible have identified events when God has acted directly and dramatically, such as Jesus rising from the dead. In addition, historians and doctors have identified times throughout history when God has acted in ways that are often identified as "supernatural," such as healing the sick. Examples, like these, throughout history have been collected by the New Testament scholar Craig Keener in his book on miracles.[4]

5. The evidence is convicting.
A final reason that many deny the evidence for a creator is its implications. For, they recognize that if they were created by God, then they are ultimately accountable to Him for their actions. They also recognize that God would likely have a great deal to say about their choices in life. However, they do not desire to live under what they view as constraints. In addition, science supports the existence of a loving, all-powerful creator who was been directly involved in

---

4. Craig Keener, *Miracles: The Credibility of the New Testament Accounts*, Baker Academic, 2011.

our world. Yet, today society is clearly in a state of turmoil and distress, which suggests that humanity has alienated itself from its creator, as described in Geneses. These facts point to the need for God to act on our behalf to restore both creation and ourselves, which naturally leads to the message of the gospel.

When some encounter this evidence, it undermines the foundation of their belief that the universe is all that exists. Once they recognize that they were created, they then have to examine their relationship with their creator. At that point the Holy Spirit can convict people's conscience about how they have violated the law God has placed in their hearts. They then have to either recognize their need for God's mercy and forgiveness, or they have to suppress that truth and accept some rationalization about how the clear evidence for design in nature is simply an illusion.

However, when anyone points out some of the specific examples mentioned above, the truth can break through their attempts at suppression. They will then either respond in anger and simply change the topic of conversation, or they will have to come to terms with their denial of God. Some will then reconsider the Gospel.

CONCLUSION

The evidence from science is one of the best ways to begin speaking about Christianity with agnostics and atheists. It dispels the myth that faith and science are in conflict as well as supports many Christian truths that are described in the Bible. As it has been stated, the book of nature is not in conflict with the book of Scripture. In addition, this evidence can challenge the very foundation of an atheists worldview, so it can grant space for them to consider the reality of God. With a little effort you can become confident in any setting to explain these basic truths that the universe had a beginning and that the evidence points to an intelligent Creator.

CLOSING DISCUSSION QUESTIONS
1. Which point in this lesson speaks to you the most?
2. Which part is easiest to grasp and remember?
3. What seems still too hard to understand?

AS A GROUP

Make a list of the intricacies and details that point to the existence of a Creator in our world and universe. Examine each item on your list and ask, "Does it take more faith to believe God created this or to believe that it somehow happened on its own?"

A MOMENT OF YOUR OWN

Complete the following prayers as you reflect on God's marvelous design and creation all around you:

Father, your eternal power and divine nature have been clearly seen since the beginning of the world (Romans 1:20). Thank you for expressing your creativity and power in the world I see and enjoy every day, in ways such as

FOLLOW UP

Read and meditate on Psalm 19. Make a list of praise to God for the wonders of nature and space. Consider the laws of science and physics that you have some knowledge of and those that stretch your understanding.

Read and meditate on Genesis 1:1-19. In what ways does nature reflect God's image?

Read and meditate on Romans 1:18-32. Visit reasons.org and begin to explore evidence of God's hand at work in conjunction with science and reason.

*Additional reading from *God's Not Dead: Evidence for God in an Age of Uncertainty:*
- Chapter 4 – There Was A Beginning

MARVEL AT THE DESIGN

KEY VERSE

"From one man he made all the nations, that they should inhabit the whole earth; and he marked out their appointed times in history and the boundaries of their lands." —Acts 17:26, NIV

KEY MOVIE QUOTE

"Evolution only tells you what happens once you have life. So where did that something that is alive come from? Well, Darwin never really addressed it. He assumed maybe some lighting hit a stagnant pool full of the right type of chemicals. Bingo, a living something. But, it is just not that simple."

KEY SCENE

Lesson four - Clip 1
             Clip 2

OPENING DISCUSSION QUESTIONS

1. What characteristics in life most demonstrate to you God's involvement?
2. How do people's views of their origin affect their perspective of life?
3. How do people's views of their origin affect their view of God?

INTRODUCTION

Most can recognize how the evidence from physics and astronomy points to a creator. However, the field of biology has often been seen as the most challenging to reconcile with Christianity. In particular, the triumph of the theory of evolution is often presented by skeptics as the knockout blow to anyone attempting to maintain an intellectually credible belief in God. Naturally, if science has proven that we are simply the product of the blind forces of nature and chance, then we can hardly be described as the creation of a loving God. However, evidence over the past few decades has increasingly identified, even in this discipline, the fingerprints of God. This shift was dramatically demonstrated in 2004 when the book entitled

There Is a God: How the World's Most Notorious Atheist Changed His Mind was published. This book is the story of Anthony Flew, who was perhaps the foremost atheistic philosopher in the world. It describes his coming to doubt atheism as the result of advances in molecular biology, particularly DNA. What most impacted Dr. Flew was that DNA contains a level of complexity that could only result from an intelligent designer. In this lesson we will cover the implications of these discoveries and realities.

PRINCIPLES OF LESSON

1. Life only comes from life.

Some of the clearest evidence for God's involvement in life comes from the study of its origin. Regardless of one's opinion on evolution, everyone recognizes that it can only explain what happens after one has life, it cannot explain how the first cell originated. Most scientists recognize that the chances of a cell spontaneously forming on the early earth are fantastically small. The typical probability cited is one chance in 10 to the power of 40,000—a number that represents a one followed by enough zeros to fill a small book. That probability is comparable to the chances of a tornado moving through a junkyard and assembling a fully operational 747 jet airplane.

Not surprisingly, most scientists recognize that a cell could never have originated by chance. Instead, they believe that somehow the laws of nature could have spontaneously brought together the different building blocks to form the first cell. Unfortunately, nature does the opposite of what is needed. First, it tends to move from order to disorder. For instance, we have to work diligently to keep our room clean, since it naturally tends to become messy. Second, nature tends to move from high energy to low energy; water runs downhill, never uphill. However, a cell is both highly ordered and contains very high energy compared to its separate building blocks. For simple chemicals to come together to form a cell, nature would need to act in the opposite direction of its normal course, much like a messy room spontaneously becomes well organized during an earthquake.

As a last ditch attempt, many skeptics argue that the sun could have supplied the energy needed to create the order in a cell. However, this idea is much like setting off a stick of dynamite under a stack of bricks and expecting the energy to create a house. Some scientists have become so challenged by this problem that they have even proposed that life was seeded on earth by aliens.

2. Life contains information.

The argument for design in life does not solely rest on the impossibility of its origin by some natural process. Certain of its characteristics are known to only result from intelligent agents, particularly the information in DNA. As a biology refresher, DNA stores the information needed to manufacture and operate every structure and system in living organisms. It consists of a language of four letters, which are identified (for short), A, T, C, and G. Different sequences of these letters in DNA are translated into the different building blocks of cells and ultimately into entire organisms. This translation is analogous to the sequences of dots and dashes in Morse code being translated into words, which combine into paragraphs. The more biologists decipher the DNA code, the more they are recognizing its complexity and ingenuity, which vastly exceeds that of even the most sophisticated computer software.

As mentioned, the letters in DNA are arranged in very specific sequences to provide the needed information to construct and operate an organism. For nature to blindly produce enough information for even a single gene would be much like a student sitting on their cell phone and accidently pocket texting the message, "Don't tell anyone, but I cheated on the test." The required ordering of letters in DNA, like the letters in a pocket text, could only result from an intelligent agent.

As another analogy, imagine boiling a pot of Campbell's alphabet soup and noticing the letters form the sentence, "I hope you feel better soon and have a nice day." Such an arrangement could not be explained by the chemistry of the pasta or the physics of the boiling water. Like the pocket text, it could only be explained by intelligence. The amount of information in even the simplest cell is the equivalent of the information contained in this lesson.

3. Life appears suddenly.

Some Christians, most notably Dr. Francis Collins, who actually mapped the human genome, have argued that Christianity and evolution are compatible. They believe that evolution was the tool that God used to create humanity in His image. However, as mentioned, discoveries in biology over the past several decades have shown that an unguided evolutionary process cannot explain the sudden appearance in the fossil record of complex life.

Darwin predicted that species change gradually over millions of years to become radically new species. For instance, he expected a species of fish to have changed over millions of years to become the first amphibian. This transition would have involved a series of countless numbers of intermediate species, each only slightly different from its predecessor. These transitional series represent the various branches on the tree of life linking all species back to the first cell. However, the actual pattern looks completely different.

Even accepting the dates of fossils given by mainstream biologists, the fossil record—the record of extinct species in the earth—does not show life gradually changing over time. Most notably, many major animal groups, such as vertebrates, all appear suddenly in an event known as the Cambrian explosion. And, this event is simply the most dramatic of a general pattern throughout the fossil record. Whenever new types of animals appear, such as the first fish or the first reptiles, they typically appear suddenly without series of identifiable ancestors. Then, after they appear, they never change significantly. As such, the entire fossil record points to God directing the unfolding of life from start to finish.

This general observation has challenged the very foundations of evolutionary theory. For instance, world experts in the fossil record from China have concluded that the pattern of nature looks nothing like Darwin expected. Dr. J. Y. Chen commented in a conference at the University of Washington on how Chinese scientists are starting to question Darwinian evolution. When one American scientist asked him to clarify, he said, "In China we can criticize Darwin, but not the government. In America, you can criticize the government, but not Darwin."[5]

4. Life demonstrates purpose.
Virtually every aspect of life reveals purpose and foresight. For instance, the eye demonstrates indescribable levels of sophistication for the specific purpose of vision. For us to see properly, countless individual pieces have to be perfectly integrated, including the cornea, lens, iris, and retina. Moreover, even completely functional eyes are useless without the nerve cords connecting them to the correct parts of the brain. And, even all of those parts are useless unless the brain has the correct wiring to properly process the signals from the millions of light sensitive cells in the retina. As mentioned, Ming Wang is one of the world's foremost experts on the eye. Part of the reason he came to believe in God was the impossibility of the eye originating from any other process than intelligent design.

The eye demonstrates a property common throughout life known as irreducible complexity. The term refers to biological structures or processes that are composed of multiple parts, where many of the parts are essential for even the most basic functionality. Such structures cannot be produced by the gradual step-by-step process of evolution since they do not work at all unless multiple parts are present. Nearly every aspect of living organisms has this property. But the classic example is a molecular machine known as the bacterial flagellum. It resides in a bacteria's cell membrane and looks like an outboard motor. It contains several precisely integrated parts, many of which must be present for the motor to work at all. In addition, each part has to attach to every other part perfectly, and assembly instructions are needed in the cell for it to be properly constructed. Such careful integration of parts for a predetermined purpose unmistakably points to an intelligent designer.

5. Human life is special.
In the nineteenth century, many were attempting to view life from the perspective that God does not exist. Influential thinkers

---

5. Meyer, Stephen C., Darwin's Doubt: The Explosive Origin of Animal Life and the Case for Intelligent Design; HarperCollins, 2013, p. 52.

embraced Darwinian evolution not only for scientific reasons, but also so they had a replacement for God's role in creation. Since that time, the theory has become solidified as the official creation narrative of Western secular civilization. As such, it is seen as a non-negotiable tenet of secular faith, so no evidence could ever convince its adherents that it was wrong. Some scientists have even openly stated that they would never consider under any circumstance the possibility of design in nature.

Due to deep philosophical attachments to Darwinian theory, Christians need to use wisdom on when and how to address the topic. For some, learning the challenges to the theory can help break them free of the false view of reality they have accepted. Others will respond with anger and refuse to listen to anything else you might desire to say. The best approach is to start with the general evidence from science described in the last lesson. Then, if they seem intrigued, you can explain the evidence related to the origin of life and the fossil record. If they then start to seriously question their entire philosophical framework, you could more directly address the key elements of the Christian faith.

Another avenue to bridge biology and Christianity is the special nature of humans. We have countless features that separate us from other species. We are unique in our ability for advanced communication. This talent alone depends on our advanced brain power, our vocal cord ability that produce such a large variety of sounds, and special regions in the brain specifically designed for language. In addition, our hands are capable of handling tools with great precision. This ability combined with our upright posture enables us to build structures and more advanced tools. All of these traits allow us to advance culturally and technologically.

CONCLUSION

The evidence for design in physics points to an all-powerful creator who exists outside of time and space. The evidence from biology reveals that God has also been intimately involved throughout the history of our world. In fact, the information in the cell demonstrates that he was involved in our creation at the level of properly arranging the atoms in our DNA. This further demonstrates that the God revealed through science matches the God of the Bible.

DISCUSSION QUESTIONS
1. Which point in this lesson speaks to you the most?
2. Which part is easiest to grasp and remember?
3. What seems still too hard to understand?

AS A GROUP
Together, make a list of facts, abilities and details that separate humans from other life on earth. What abilities do humans have that other animals and plants do not?

A MOMENT OF YOUR OWN
Complete the following prayers as you reflect on God's marvelous design within and around you:

God, you have woven me together with fascinating precision and detail. "I praise you because I am fearfully and wonderfully made" (Psalm 139:14). Thank you for giving me the gift of life and for allowing my body, mind and soul be able to forgive my complaints and comparisons about myself. Please replace my insecurities of

_____

_____

with your truths that you wove me together according to your purposes and that in you, I am

_____

_____

FOLLOW UP

Read and meditate on Psalm 139. Make a list of thanks to God for the wonders of human life and the details of design He has woven and expressed in your own life.

Read and meditate on Genesis 1:20-31. In what ways does humanity reflect God's image on earth?

Read Acts 17:16-34. What were the prevailing worldviews that Paul was addressing? How would you describe his tone and approach in presenting God's truth?

Meditate on Acts 17:24-28. What is your worldview? List the guiding principles that serve as the foundation for your belief and action. Think about where these ideas have come from. How and why have you adopted them? Where do they guide you?

*Additional reading from *God's Not Dead: Evidence for God in an Age of Uncertainty:*
- Chapter 5 – Life Is No Accident
- Chapter 6 – Life Has Meaning And Purpose

UNDERSTAND GOD'S PURPOSE

KEY VERSE

"This is the message we have heard from Him (Jesus) and declare to you: God is light; in Him there is no darkness at all." —1 John 1:5, NIV

KEY MOVIE QUOTE

"Evil is atheism's most potent weapon against the Christian faith."

KEY SCENE

Lesson five - Clip 1

OPENING DISCUSSION QUESTIONS

1. How do different people's encounters with tragedy affect their response to God, such as the main characters in the movie?
2. What do many people believe is the source of evil in the world?
3. How would you explain the purpose of life from a Christian perspective?

INTRODUCTION

This final classroom scene where Josh and Professor Radisson go head to head about evil and suffering is indeed memorable. The tension is felt every time I watch this dramatic encounter. Josh has been respectful and restrained in all of his dealings with his persecutor, but he matches his professor's attacks with the boldness of the Lord. The issue of evil and suffering is still the most emotionally charged area of the debate in terms of talking about God's existence.

Think about it ... eventually, even scientists the earth will cease to exist, and the universe will end up as lifeless matter floating through space. Any sense of meaning and purpose that could be mustered will amount to nothing more than a pitiful act of self-deception.

Some skeptics have proposed that people should create their own meaning and purpose. However, defining ones purpose is much like writing oneself a million dollar check. It might make a person feel like they have something of genuine value. However, if that check is not backed by something real, when they attempt to cash it, they will quickly recognize its worthlessness. Anyone who does not base their purpose on God's revelation will eventually come to the same conclusion when they stand before Him to give an account for their life.

In addition, skeptics can never meaningfully challenge injustice or oppression, for without God, people have no intrinsic value. In addition, if people are unconcerned about the possibility of facing a final judgment, all restraints would be removed and they would unleash the full evil in their hearts. Without God there is no objective basis to differentiate good from evil. Any sense of morality is simply a byproduct of humanity's evolutionary development. Therefore, the choice between helping the poor and oppressing the poor would be no less arbitrary than the choice between having crunchy peanut butter or smooth peanut butter for lunch. Only by recognizing God can we objectively differentiate right from wrong. Only because of God, evil and suffering will not have the last word.

PRINCIPLES OF LESSON

1. Evil is a choice—it's the risk God took in making us in His image.
The problem of evil is one of the greatest challenges to the Christian faith. The very existence of evil brings into question how God could be both all-powerful and good.

There is no diminishing the enormous pain and suffering that exists. Whether it's something as horrific as the Holocaust where more than six million Jewish people were murdered, or the terrorist attacks on 9/11, there is no shortage of evil in the world. This was not God's original intention. He created the world as good, where people were to live in harmony and fellowship with Him and one another. He gave mankind the choice to either trust and obey Him, or to reject His authority and attempt to be their own god. Therefore, He gave us freedom to choose for ourselves the difference between right and wrong and to decide our own purpose. People chose the latter—an event known as the "fall" of humanity—resulting in alienation with God, each other, and creation. Since people no longer received God's perfect love and security, we fell into increasing levels of alienation and darkness.

As mankind expanded into the world in this broken state, oppression, violence, and cruelty continued to grow. Therefore, the evil in the world today is not due to God's lack of power or goodness, it is the result of His giving humanity the power to choose and we chose to reject Him. Today, we have the same choice. We can either turn to God or continue to live according to our own rules and instincts. Unfortunately, most still decide to ignore God's guidelines and often act selfishly, unkindly, and unwisely. Then, they and others experience the consequences.

Skeptics rightly point out that many who claim to believe in God and His laws have perpetuated as much evil as those without faith. However, this fact does not discredit God or Christianity. Jesus himself said that many would call themselves His disciples, but would not follow His commands. Just because I believe in the police and such a thing as the speed limit, doesn't mean I guarantee not to speed. In the same way, just because someone knows God exists doesn't guarantee he'll keep His laws. Ultimately, the existence of evil doesn't point to the absence of God from the world, but the absence of God from our lives.

2. No God—No Evil

As mentioned, skeptics have no objective standard for morality, so from their perspective, evil cannot exist. As the Russian writer Dostoevsky said, "Without God, all things are permissible." However, most recognize that real standards for good and evil do exist. This reality becomes starkly evident when studying the atrocities that have taken place throughout history. In fact, many of the worst examples were the result of people embodying an ethic that reflected the Darwinian idea of survival of the fittest. Skeptics, such as Richard Dawkins, often claim society should rise above our evolutionary instincts, but they have no reason or standard to make such a claim. As C. S. Lewis stated, "How would I know the line is crooked if I didn't know what a straight line is?"

To further illustrate why objective morality depends on belief in a Creator, imagine finding a rock on the beach. Since that rock did not come with an instruction manual, you would not possess guidelines on the purpose for which you should use it. On the other hand, since a car was designed by an engineer, it comes with an owner's manual describing how to use it to its greatest capacity. If someone did not wish to follow the manual, they could create their own guidelines, such as putting water in the gas tank. However, such violations of the designer's instructions would cause the car to break down and to cease operating effectively. In the same way, since we are created by God, He knows how we are meant to operate best. Therefore, following His guidelines brings us the greatest wellbeing and helps us live purposeful lives.

As a second example, imagine someone who owns a watch, but he has no idea how to use it. That person might use it to stir a cup of tea or hammer a nail. Not only would the watch not be used to its full capacity as an instrument for keeping time, it would likely become broken. In like manner, if we do not understand that our purpose is to know and serve our Creator, we will focus our lives on meaningless distractions. Or, we will make idols out of relationships, our career, or some other temporal item. Eventually, such obsessions could easily lead to emotional stress, relational breakdown, and depression. And, these debilitating conditions often lead to destructive patterns that harm others in a never-ending domino effect of societal breakdown.

3. Morality is built-in to humanity.

As C. S. Lewis described in the book *Mere Christianity,* most people have an inward sense that objective moral standards do exist. In other words, good and evil are not illusions. Lewis pointed out that if all mankind possesses a sense of morality, it points to a moral authority behind it. Therefore, another key piece of evidence for God is the sense of right and wrong and good and evil that He put in all of us. Most religious systems have identified very similar moral principles, since those principles correspond to the reality of how God designed people, as well as societies, to function. What's funny is that those who claim there are not objective moral standards expect others to treat them justly and fairly. They also often argue for human rights and equality for woman and minorities to be promoted even in nations with conflicting cultural values. Yet where do these morals come from?

Skeptics often argue that they can still act ethically without religion or belief in God. However, the reason that they have any instinctive desire to act morally is due to their being created in God's image. It's because God made us all that we all share this common set of moral standards, regardless of culture or context. Professor Radisson tries to use this in his debate with Josh by accusing him of saying that a person needs God to be good. Josh responds by saying that without God, why should we be good? If we are just animals, and there is no ultimate purpose, then what basis do we have to make moral judgments?

We all know that such behaviors as kindness, mercy, equality, and forgiveness are true and good because we were brought up in a culture deeply shaped by Christian values for hundreds of years. In contrast, when any civilization has rejected belief in any power higher than themselves, they invariably degenerate into authoritarian states with little concern for human rights. The twentieth century was the bloodiest century in human history. This was partly a result of nations attempting to live without God and rewrite the laws that defined good and evil. The failure of the Communists and the Nazi's in the last century points to the fact that mankind can no more live without God than we can live without air.

As the Bible states, *"In Him we live and move and have our being."*
—Acts 17:28, NIV

4. God has a plan to remove evil.
When I was on an airplane once, a man sitting in seat 14D told me he was an atheist because he felt that the existence of evil meant a good God couldn't exist. I told him, "God could remove all the evil in the world in an instant. All He had to do was kill every person and evil would stop." This seemed to get his attention. I then told him that God had a plan to remove evil from the world by changing the human heart where evil resides. I explained to him that God's plan extracts evil without destroying the person. Thus His plan is

to remove evil from the world one person at a time. As we will see in the last week of this study, that is the hope of the gospel. In fact, I told the man that God wanted to remove the evil from the world "starting in seat 14D." Sadly, he wanted all the evil in the world to vanish, but he wasn't willing to surrender his own evil.

People typically desire God to stop others from doing evil, but they don't wish for God to impinge upon their own freedom to do whatever they desire. They really want evil to stop happening to them, but not through them.

However, whenever anyone puts their faith in Christ's work on the cross to defeat the power of evil, God begins to remove the darkness in their hearts and restore them to their full humanity. God will remove all evil from the world at the final judgment, but He has already started the process through the gospel. When we turn to Jesus, the Holy Spirit reshapes our hearts, so our driving motivations shift from primarily serving ourselves and advancing our own agendas to serving others. Then we can help turn back the evil from the world.

Throughout history, when Christians recommitted their lives to serving Christ and prayed for their cities, God would manifest His presence to such an extent that cities would be transformed. For instance, crime would all but disappear, mercy ministries would flourish to help the needy, and people would treat each other with kindness and respect. At times, these revivals would spread around the world. Unfortunately, people would eventually become distracted and turn their focus away from God and fall back into darkness.

5) God will judge evil.
Eventually according to the Scriptures, God will remove all of the evil in the world at the final judgment. There will be an end to the current world and a final accounting for all that has been done both good and bad. As the Apostle Paul wrote, *"We must all appear before the judgment seat of Christ, so that each of us may receive what is due us for the things done while in the body whether good or bad"* (2 Corinthians 5:10, NIV).

This produces a deep sense of the fear of the Lord. This is the good kind of fear. Like cholesterol, there is good fear and bad fear. The bad fear is the kind that Christ has delivered us from. However, the good kind is the fear of the Lord that makes us run from evil (Proverbs 16:6).

In our society today it is the knowledge that we will give an accounting to the authorities for our finances as well as our actions that causes evil to be restrained. Just like the police and the court system punish evil, God will one day do the same.

This kind of judgment isn't contrary to God's love and mercy, but it is because of His love and compassion. God isn't unjust because He allows evil to exist. This again is because He has allowed mankind to have a real right to choose good or evil. God would only be unjust if He allowed evil to go unpunished. According to the Scripture, the fact that Christ has been raised from the dead proves that He has been appointed by God to judge the world (Acts 17:31).

The good news is that God has provided a way to be forgiven and cleansed from all our sin because of Christ's death on the cross. God's patience is giving time for people to choose to turn to Him before the judgment is enacted.

Understanding the nature of that judgment helps us understand Christ's work on the cross. Many feel that God's judgment will look something like a scale, where one's good deeds will be compared to one's bad deeds. However, when God restores creation, He cannot allow any evil into it, for even the smallest amount would start the cycle of corruption again. Therefore, we can never earn our way into God's Kingdom through our good works. For that reason, Jesus died on the cross to pay the penalty for our sin and to defeat the power of evil in our lives. When we have faith in and submit to him, our life connects to his perfect life. Then God's power begins a transformative process making us like Him, which is completed at His second coming. Then we can spend eternity in God's presence in a world brought to its full intended potential.

CONCLUSION
"How can you hate someone if they don't exist?"

Skeptics often attempt to use the existence of evil and suffering as an attack against Christianity. However, denying God does not take away the pain. It just takes away the hope. Only the Christian faith provides the true explanation for the root cause. It also provides the resources today to defeat it personally and socially. And, it provides the only hope to ultimately remove it. The existence of evil doesn't demonstrate God's absence from the world, but His absence from our hearts. God is the one who defines evil: He tells us what it is. He denounces evil: He tells us to choose good and not evil; and finally, He defeated evil through His death on the cross and His resurrection.

DISCUSSION QUESTIONS
1. How might you help the people you know better understand the nature of evil in the world and how the Christian faith offers real hope?
2. How would you explain the need for God to justify objective morality?
3. How would you explain that, without God, life has no meaning or purpose?

AS A GROUP
Make two evil lists side by side. In the first column, write common complaints about evil that people use to blame, discount or doubt God. In the second column, write ways that God offers and enacts hope to overcome evil. Consider Bible verses and personal examples.

A MOMENT OF YOUR OWN
Complete the following prayers.

Father, thank you that you are "close to the brokenhearted and save those who are crushed in spirit" (Psalm 34:18, NIV). Thank you that you know the hurt and brokenness I have experienced, such as_____

Please continue to remind me _____

_____

and to fill me with hope in your plans for my future (Jeremiah 29:11).

Father, when I am discouraged, help me to remember that you have overcome the evil and trouble in this world (John 16:32-33). Thank you for healing and overcoming evil in my life by _____

_____

FOLLOW UP
Read and meditate on Romans 8:28. Make a list of ways you have seen God turn suffering into good in your life and in the lives of your friends and loved ones.

Read and think about Romans 8:38-39. Contrast the hope that Jesus offers with the hopelessness that exists if there is no God.

Read 2 Corinthians 1:3-4. Who do you know who is struggling without hope in Christ? List three ways you can show compassion, love and hope to them.

*Additional reading from *God's Not Dead: Evidence for God in an Age of Uncertainty:*
  • Chapter 3 – God And Evil Are No Illusions

SHARE THE MESSAGE

KEY VERSE

"Christ died for our sins according to the Scripture, that He was buried, that He was raised on the third day according to the Scriptures."
—1 Corinthians 15:3–4, NIV

KEY MOVIE QUOTE

"Do you know Jesus?" —Pastor Dave to Professor Radisson as he is dying.

KEY SCENE

Lesson six - Clip 1

OPENING DISCUSSION QUESTIONS

1. Have you ever shared the gospel with a stranger?
2. Has learning the evidence for God's existence given you greater confidence to engage an unbeliever in a spiritual conversation?
3. Do you think you can be bold in your witness while being gentle and respectful at the same time?

INTRODUCTION TO THE LESSON

While preparation is vital to becoming an effective witness for Christ, at some point, we need to step out and start sharing the gospel. In addition to praying for opportunities, you can adjust your schedule so you can connect more often and more deeply with people outside the church. For instance, you can become involved in activities or join organizations with diverse participants. Moreover, you can cultivate the lifestyle of hospitality. As you get involved with people who don't know the Lord, they will inevitably see the centrality of Jesus that marks your life, which will result in sincere questions about the difference your faith has made. Those questions will lead to meaningful spiritual conversations.

At first, you can defend the existence of God. Remember, knowing that God exists is the beginning of faith. Then, you can explain how He created the world as well as mankind. This knowledge should result in a desire on people's part to begin to seek God. This can lead to the opportunity for you to explain the Christian story that is expressed in the gospel. There is no greater privilege than to communicate that message to unbelievers. As the Apostle Paul said, *"We are therefore Christ's ambassadors as though God were making His appeal through us. We implore you on Christ's behalf, be reconciled to God."* —2 Corinthians 5:20, NIV

When people respond to the gospel, you can then connect them with the Christian community, and help them on the first stages of their spiritual growth.

PRINCIPLES OF LESSON

1. Understand the gospel.

Before you can share the gospel, you need to understand it. A brief summary is as follows:

God became man in Jesus Christ. He lived the life we should have lived and died the death we should have died, in our place. Three days later He rose from the dead proving that He is the Son of God and offering the gift of salvation to everyone who will repent and believe in Him.

You should memorize this gospel summary so you can present it on a moment's notice.

Let's look briefly at the key aspects of this summary.

God became man in Jesus Christ.

The Creator of the universe came to earth in the form of Jesus Christ. This is the greatest mystery of all time—that God would enter His own creation in order to rescue mankind. Some try to simply say that Jesus was a great teacher or even a prophet. However, He claimed to be the Lord. As C. S. Lewis said, "Jesus was either a liar because He claimed to be the son of God and knew He wasn't, or He was a lunatic who thought He was the son of God, or He was indeed the Lord. You can't simply call Him a good man."

He lived the life we should have lived.

Jesus perfectly obeyed the moral law of God. He was without sin. The original intention was for mankind to obey God's laws. Through disobedience and rebellion we fell into the darkness and grip of sin. Christ's perfect obedience as a man of God's law qualified Him to represent us before God.

And died the death we should have died, in our place.

Because of sin, we deserved punishment. If there is no penalty for breaking God's laws, then they cease to be laws and become merely suggestions. Jesus Christ became our substitute by offering His perfect life as a sacrifice for our sins.

Three days later He rose from the dead, proving He is the Son of God.

The resurrection of Jesus from the dead verified that He indeed was who He said He was. When people ask how you can know that Jesus Christ is truly the only way to God, you can confidently stand on His resurrection as the proof of that claim.

He offers salvation for those who repent and believe in Him.

The gospel calls us to put our faith in Christ. To have faith means to trust and obey what He says is true. To repent means to turn from trusting in our own efforts, as well as to be sorry for our sinful ways. As you turn to Christ and trust in Him, He promises to give you new life.

2. Believe the gospel.

"For God so loved the world that He gave His one and only Son, that whoever believes in Him shall not perish but have eternal life."
—John 3:16, NIV

Next, we need to believe the gospel deeply. As we learned in the earlier lessons, real faith isn't blind. We have been given overwhelming evidence that God is real and that Jesus Christ is His Son. Though we don't claim to have all the answers, we have enough evidence to commit ourselves to believe what God has promised us. We should know that the resurrection demonstrates that Jesus is the Son of God. We also know that Jesus' words are true and our sins are forgiven. What a wonderful magnificent promise to know that Christ has paid the price for our sins. The prophet Isaiah spoke of this almost seven hundred years before Christ when he said that He would be *"pierced for our transgressions and crushed for our iniquities ... and by His wounds we are healed"* (Isaiah 53:5, NIV). All of the guilt and shame has been removed from us, and we now stand free and blameless in God's sight. We are called children of God! There is nothing on this earth that can compare with this free gift from God. As a third-year student at college, this message came to me and I reached out and believed it like someone in the desert dying of thirst. Even though my friends and family didn't understand what I was going through, they knew that my faith was genuine and sincere. More than thirty years later, it is still as real and powerful to me as it was then.

By believing the gospel, we experience the promise Jesus gave us of a new birth. As He said to a religious leader named Nicodemus, *"You must be born again"* —John 3:7, NIV. This new life is obviously spiritual, not physical. We become new on the inside. *"Therefore if anyone is in Christ, the new creation has come: the old has gone, the new is here!"* —2 Corinthians 5:17, NIV.

When we believe the message, this promised transformation takes place. That doesn't mean we don't have struggles, temptations, and setbacks, but we have a new source of strength inside of us.

When these truths penetrate our hearts, they shape our speech, our decisions, our emotions, and our motivations. It is this confidence that marked the early followers of Christ.

In my own life, this confidence I possessed resulted in my family and many of my friends coming to faith as well. This is the greatest hope and dream of everyone who understands and believes the gospel.

3) Share the gospel.
"How can they call on the one they have not believed in? And how can they believe in the one of whom they have not heard? And how can they hear without someone preaching to them?" —Romans 10:14, (NIV)

It has become a popular statement to say "preach the gospel, and if necessary, use words." Make no mistake, it is necessary to use words! The word gospel comes from a Greek word that means "good news." Who has ever heard of good news that isn't shared with others? As you look at the Scriptures, it is evident that men and women understand that it was their responsibility and privilege to communicate the message to the world around them. Jesus' final words to His disciples were, *Therefore go and make disciples of all nations ...*" —Matthew 28:19, NIV

There are many reasons people use to avoid this responsibility. Many times it comes down to fear. The best way to overcome this fear of talking about God is to simply start stepping out in faith to initiate conversations. It is a challenge to learn to talk to others in a way that is not awkward or offensive. To overcome this obstacle, we offer you a simple strategy called S.A.L.T. This acronym stands for: **S**tart a conversation; **A**sk questions; **L**isten; and **T**ell the story. Starting the conversation can sometimes be the most difficult step. However, learning to ask questions can take a lot of the awkwardness out of the entire process of sharing the gospel. While people are speaking and answering the questions you ask, do not interrupt them, but instead, listen sincerely to their answers. You'll be amazed at what they will tell you; and by listening respectfully, they will often listen to you when you speak. Time and time again following this simple strategy has turned gospel conversations from negative to very positive experiences for all involved. In fact, many times skeptics will thank you for not being belligerent and actually listening to their answers before you share your beliefs.

To help guide this process, we have developed a tool known as The God Test (TheGodTest.org). It is a two-sided pamphlet with a separate set of questions on each side. The conversation starter question is: "Do you believe in God?" If they say no, then you turn to **Side A**, and ask them the ten questions that are designed for atheists or agnostics. If they say they believe in God, then you turn to **Side B**, and ask a different set of ten questions. These questions draw out a person's foundational beliefs, such as their understanding of God, morality, and the meaning of life. Their answers to these questions help them confront the most significant questions about life, and help you learn to engage in these kinds of discussions with grace and ease.[6]

6. For more information about The God Test, go to www.thegodtest.org.

4. The gospel is the power of God.

I had a conversation with a young man who had walked away from the his religious upbringing and had become a psychic, reading peoples palms and telling their fortunes on the streets of New Orleans. I started the conversation by asking him how and why he was involved in this. I listened intently for almost fifteen minutes while he answered my questions. I could feel the pain that he had experienced and desperately wanted to help him. After I had asked several questions and listened without correcting him or arguing with him, he asked me, "Tell me why you do what you do." I paused and said, "I preach the gospel because it is the only thing on this planet that can tell a person what is really wrong with them."

I then told him the story of my wife being sick for more than two years with a mysterious ailment no doctor could detect. When we finally found out what was really wrong with her, it was good news! Now we could start treating the real problem. Because of this, she is healthy today. The gospel is like an MRI for the soul that shows the source of people's individual problems, and the challenges in society that result from their broken relationships with God. It also gives us the true cure that can heal our wounds. When anyone seeks to anchor their identity in anything other than the true God, they inevitably experience insecurity, uncertainty, and dysfunction.

There are countless voices promising to help us fix our problems. Only within Christianity is the cure really found—our value and acceptance by God rest on Jesus' perfect life and sacrifice. The experience of God's love empowers and motivates us to live according to God's guidelines, which results in an abundant life as we seek to fulfill and eternal purpose. As we are transformed into new people, we can then confront the problems in our society such as racism, injustice, and poverty. As we share the gospel, that power can then change others, which can eventually transform entire communities.

5. The gospel produces good works.

On a regular basis, tragedy and crisis strike our world—whether natural disasters such as hurricanes, floods, and tornadoes, or personal tragedy and loss.

It is the love and mercy shown by the followers of Christ that have historically made a huge difference in the lives of those that are hurting. Pain and suffering are indeed a mystery and a stumbling block to many who are searching for answers in the midst of confusion. However the love and sacrifice shown by believers can help take away that pain and bring real peace and comfort.

As we have learned in this study, it is necessary to share the words of Life with others. At the same time, the power of preaching the gospel in word should coincide with the witness of our lives in deed. We should serve others and teach people practical Christian truth, such as the power of forgiveness. As believers, we should help each other to sincerely model Jesus' teaching and love to each other. We should invite those we talk to and befriend into our community so they can see Christians truly care for each other.

As a Christian, you invite others into small groups focused on practical issues, such as marriage, finances, or relationships. As they experience biblical truth practically impacting their lives, they will likely desire to understand the full Christian story. You could also invite them to join in mercy ministries, such as helping the homeless. When they participate in God's work of serving the world around them, they experience a joy that no other event or experience can bring.

For instance, identify the talents God has given you, then use them to His glory, such as painting or dance or business management. Others will see the joy in your heart and naturally wish to know its source. Moreover, as you allow God to bring restoration in the broken areas of your heart, you can become a conduit to bring similar restoration to others' hearts. Then, you will find ample opportunities to introduce people to God who transformed your life.

CONCLUSION

For many, deciding to participate with God in evangelism often transforms a mundane faith into a life-changing adventure with God. They find God answering their prayers more clearly. They also experience His presence more dramatically, and they see their spiritual gifts activated more powerfully. Most importantly, they see God use their lives to make an internal impact in others' lives. The first steps can be challenging, but with perseverance you will eventually see fruit that endures.

DISCUSSION QUESTIONS

1. What are your greatest obstacles toward being a witness for Christ? How can you overcome them?
2. What do you most need to become an effective witness: courage, knowledge, wisdom, power? How should you pray for God to assist you to gain what you need?
3. What opportunities might you be missing where you could be a witness?

AS A GROUP

As part of the S.A.L.T. acronym, listening is key to guiding meaningful spiritual conversations. Together, make a list of genuine questions you can ask to understand another person's needs and spiritual perspectives.

A MOMENT OF YOUR OWN

Complete these prayers:

Father, thank you for your patience with me and you willingness always to listen. Fill me with care and compassion for others. Help me to be "quick to listen" (James 1:19) to

by

Jesus, your death and resurrection are the ultimate hope for the world! Fill me with your courage to not be "ashamed of the gospel" (Romans 1:16) but to bring the message of your power and salvation to these friends who need you: _____

FOLLOW UP

Read John 3:16-18. Reflect on your life in light of the power of these verses. What do they mean to you? How have you responded in your beliefs and lifestyle?

Read Matthew 7:16 and Galatians 5:22-23. What traits characterize your life? What do others see and receive from you?

Go to The GodTest.Org and download the study guide to walk through the process of sharing the gospel with others.

*Additional reading from *God's Not Dead: Evidence for God in an Age of Uncertainty:*
- Chapter 10 – Living Proof
- Conclusion – Seeking God

CONCLUSION | JOIN THE MOVEMENT

The message of the movie continues to spread around the world. *God's Not Dead* is not just being texted to friends, but people just like you are learning to give reasons for the truth of this statement. Completing this six-week study is an excellent start. Now, we want you to take the next steps to become a strong defender of the faith.

When I first met with the producers of the movie, we discussed the crisis of faith that exists on the university and high-school campuses of the world. The reports of young people abandoning their faith were deeply disturbing. At the time I was writing the book *God's Not Dead,* which gives the specific evidence people need to defend what they knew in their hearts was true, we all agreed that something bigger was at stake than making a movie and writing a book—a generation was indeed at risk and needed to be reached.

Since the release of both the book and the movie, a phenomenon has taken place. Theaters were packed for weeks as audiences cheered, cried, and clapped their hands. In a world of unbelief and bad news, the movie gave Christians something to cheer about. Thousands of people have tweeted about it, posted on Facebook, or simply called a friend and asked them to go see the movie. I spoke to a man in his 80s who told me he had seen the movie five times!

I've had the privilege of traveling to many countries to see the movie premiered. In places that people expected the movie to be ignored, such as England, it has made an impact. People are returning to God and bringing their friends, classmates, and even their critics with them.

So what are the next steps you can take to become a defender of the faith?

1. Read the book *"God's Not Dead."* The movie and this study guide have gotten you started—don't stop! The book gives nine evidences for the existence of God and goes into much greater detail than we've been able to go through in this study guide.

2. Get trained to be a defender of the faith. We are committed to help you learn to be the "Josh" in your world. We are partnering with local churches and campus ministries to continue to create the tools and the inspiration to turn this momentum into a movement that changes the world.

3. Start a class in your church or on your campus. You can begin to reach out to others and share the knowledge that you have. Remember, one of the verses of Scripture that Pastor Dave gave Josh: *"Everyone to whom much was given, of him much will be required, and from him to whom they entrusted much, they will demand the more"* (Luke 12:48, ESV).

4. Keep in touch—we want to hear your stories and help encourage you in your journey with Christ.

ADDITIONAL RESOURCES

THE GOD TEST—An apologetics and evangelism tool that helps you easily start conversations about faith, skepticism, and the meaning of life. TheGodTest.org

THE POACHED EGG—an excellent blog that brings you the best of the articles, blogs, and video's from around the world of apologetics and evangelism. ThePoachedEgg.Org

EVERY NATION CAMPUS—an international campus organization that presents the gospel to college students, and helps disciple them in the faith. EveryNation.org

RATIO CHRISTI—(Reason of Christ) an international apologetics organization that focuses on equipping college students to defend the faith. RatioChristi.org

REASONABLE FAITH—this is the teaching ministry of Dr. William Lane Craig. Dr. Craig is considered one of the leading defenders of the Christian faith in the world. ReasonableFaith.org

REASONS TO BELIEVE—is a group of scientists that give reasons that science points to the God of the Bible. RTB is led by astronomer Dr. Hugh Ross. Reasons.org

DR. JOHN LENNOX—he was referenced in the movie as a mathematician and philosopher. Dr. Lennox teaches at Oxford, and has debated the most prominent atheists in the world on the existence of God. JohnLennox.org

DAN WALLACE—considered one of the most prominent Christian voices on the reliability of the Bible. He leads the Center for the Study of New Testament Manuscripts. CSNTM.org

DISCOVERY INSTITUTE—focuses on advancing the dialogue on faith, science, and culture. Dr. Stephen Meyer is a vital voice in the discussion on Intelligent Design (ID). Discovery.org/CSC

GOD'S NOT DEAD

GETTING STARTED

Thank you for choosing the *God's Not Dead: What Do You Believe?* DVD-Based Study. Our prayer is that in the next six weeks, you and your group members will:

- Develop a better understanding of who Jesus is.
- Go deeper in your relationship with Jesus
- Discover God's plan for mankind

This small-group leader's guide will focus your attention on the DVD-based study, the resources inside the kit, and how to use them successfully.

Below are steps you can take to have a successful group experience with *God's Not Dead: What Do You Believe?*

STEPS FOR SUCCESS

1. Read this small-group leader's guide.
It will give you an overview of *God's Not Dead: What Do You Believe?* and provide guidance for leading discussions with your group. This guide includes information on the themes in the movie *God's Not Dead* and how you can use the film with this study.

2. Review the *God's Not Dead: What Do You Believe? Study Guide.*
Review the study guide to become familiar with each week's small-group study and discussion questions.

3. Invite people to join your group.
Even if you already have an established group with plenty of members, *God's Not Dead: What Do You Believe?* provides you with an opportunity to invite other people to join you. There are many

in your community who are searching for joy and purpose in their lives, but they don't know the truth about Jesus Christ.

Prayerfully consider whom you might invite to join your *God's Not Dead: What Do You Believe?* DVD-based study and encourage your current members to do the same. Your invitations could make an eternal difference!

4. Communicate with your group members.

Contact your group members to let them know when your meetings will start and what to expect. Determine whether your church is providing a *God's Not Dead: What Do You Believe? Study Guide* for each small-group member, if you're going to purchase the book for your members and have them reimburse you, or whether your members will purchase the study guide on their own.

Once you begin your sessions, communicate with your members every week—to encourage them, remind them of the weekly insights, and provide prayer and support.

The *God's Not Dead: What Do You Believe? Study Guide*

The *God's Not Dead: What Do You Believe? Study Guide* is a key element in the overall study. It is designed to correspond and work with the *God's Not Dead: What Do You Believe?* DVD-Based Study by teaching each person in your group terrific lessons, both through your group discussion and with individual exercises that follow each session.

The study guide was written to help participants discover what they believe and how to take a stand for their beliefs.

What Is the *God's Not Dead: What Do You Believe? Study?*

The *God's Not Dead: What Do You Believe?* DVD-based study is a six-week study designed to help everyone—those who are new to the faith and those who have been believers for many years—discover what they believe and how to stand for it. Based on clips from the film *God's Not Dead*, the study includes everything you need to grow deeper in your relationship with God and your friends and have the courage to stand up for what you believe.

There are six themes covered:
- **GET PREPARED** – Learn and know the evidence for the existence of God through the truth of His word and the world He made.
- **HAVE NO FEAR** – Be confident as you step out and share the reasons to believe.
- **EMBRACE THE EVIDENCE** – The beginning of the universe points to a creator.
- **MARVEL AT THE DESIGN** – The complexity of life points to an intelligent Designer.
- **UNDERSTAND GOD'S PURPOSE** – Making sense of evil and suffering in a broken world.
- **SHARE THE MESSAGE** – Start the adventure of sharing God's truth to the world around you.

For all six of these themes there are both small-group discussion questions and individual exercises in *The God's Not Dead: What Do You Believe? Study Guide* to help your group go deeper into the scripture and into your relationships.

The following is an example of the things you will discover and learn how to practice on your journey through this study:
- Discover your greatest obstacle in taking a stand for Jesus.
- Learn how to rise up and boldly proclaim your faith to a hurting world.
- Become confident in explaining the basic truths of creation and the Creator.
- Have a better understanding of the nature of evil in the world and how the Christian faith offers real hope.
- See His presence more dramatically in your life and how it affects others.

Finally, the life-changing benefit each participant will derive from this study will depend, in large part, on each individual's desire and determination to discover and put into practice the truths and insights they receive.

GUIDELINES FOR LEADING A SMALL GROUP OR CLASS

Leaders cast a vision.
Leaders are critical to the success of any group. As a small-group or class leader, your enthusiasm and example can inspire your members to:
- consistently attend group meetings
- openly participate in discussions
- faithfully complete individual lessons
- draw closer to God
- invite others to join your group

Pray for the requests shared by the group members during the week. Cast a vision for your group! Those who follow you will rise only as high as the expectations you set, so cast a vision of complete participation.

Leaders follow God.
"David said to the Philistine, 'You come against me with sword and spear and javelin, but I come against you in the name of the LORD Almighty, the God of the armies of Israel, whom you have defied.'"
—1 Samuel 17:45, NIV

Leading a group can be time-consuming, but be sure to set aside enough quiet time for you to be strengthened and encouraged by God. The foundation for your leadership will come from the peace and wisdom you find in your own relationship with God.

Leaders pray.
"As for me, far be it from me that I should sin against the LORD by failing to pray for you. And I will teach you the way that is good and right."
—1 Samuel 12:23, NIV

Pray for guidance about who to invite to your group and for God to encourage their participation. Once your group begins, ask for prayer requests and encourage all of your members to pray for each other. God's mighty hand moves in response to our prayers!

Leaders encourage.
"In all my prayers for all of you, I always pray with joy because of your partnership in the gospel from the first day until now, being confident of this, that he who began a good work in you will carry it on to completion until the day of Christ Jesus." —Philippians 1:4–6, NIV

Encourage your members to come to each weekly session, be involved, pray, and complete the daily readings in the *God's Not Dead: What Do You Believe? Study Guide* so they will get the most out of this DVD-based study. Encourage them to be receptive to God continuing His work in them and in their families.

Leaders invite and include.
"I have become all things to all people so that by all possible means I might save some." —1 Corinthians 9:22, NIV

The *God's Not Dead: What Do You Believe? DVD-Based Study* is intended for both Christians and those who have not yet entered into a relationship with Christ. This study has the power to help them experience God's amazing love for them and help them study God's Word. At the end of the six weeks, they will have been encouraged to draw closer to God and to leave a godly legacy behind for the next generation.

Pray for God to bring to your mind the names of people you can invite to your group. Be conscious of how to make new members feel comfortable and welcome at each session. Encourage your members to invite their friends and neighbors to join them in the group.

As you lead each session, be sensitive to personality types (i.e., introvert and extrovert). Gently draw out quieter members by asking nonthreatening questions. Talkative members may need to be gently reminded to allow everyone to participate.

Guidelines for your group
During your first session, review group guidelines with your

participants. See some suggested guidelines below. You can read these to your group, or write your own guidelines using these as a starting point.

- **Priority:** Make the group meeting a priority in your schedule. If you are unable to attend or are running late, contact the group leader.
- **Preparedness:** Prepare for the lesson each week and come ready to share. What you put into the lesson is what you'll get out of it.
- **Participation:** Participate in the discussion, but keep answers brief so others may share as well.
- **Respect:** Remember that everyone has a right to their opinion, and all questions are encouraged and respected. Listen attentively to others without interrupting them.
- **Confidentiality:** Anything of a personal nature that is said in the meeting should not be repeated outside the meeting. This group is intended to be a safe place for open discussion and sharing.
- **Honesty:** Strive to be real and honest as you share with the group. If you have suggestions about how to improve the group sessions, discuss them with the leader.
- **Connectedness:** Seek to know and care for other group members, as well as share transparently regarding your own emotional, spiritual, and physical needs.
- **Support:** Actively support the mission and values of the small group and refrain from gossip and criticism. Communicate directly and privately with anyone with whom you have an issue.

GOD'S NOT DEAD:
WHAT DO YOU BELIEVE?
STUDY GUIDE

FORMAT AND SCHEDULE

The *God's Not Dead: What Do You Believe? DVD-Based Study* is organized as described below.

Introduction

This gives some basic information on the study that will familiarize you and your group members with each of the sections of the study guide and their purpose.

God's Not Dead Movie

Going to see the *God's Not Dead* movie or showing it in your church or youth group, is a great way to kick off a new small group, or a new session for your existing group. Even if some or all of the members of your group have seen the movie, watching it together will give you an opportunity to catch details you missed in the first showing. And, seeing the film together is a great start for a thought-provoking discussion on what's really valuable in life.

Small-Group Session

During your weekly study, your group will watch the video clip(s) for that week's theme. This is located on the Resource DVD in the *God's Not Dead: What Do You Believe? DVD-Based Study Kit*. Your group will then open the *God's Not Dead: What Do You Believe? Study Guide*—so you'll want them to bring their own guide and turn to that week's session.

You will all read the Scripture passage and answer some questions relating to the short video clip(s) you just watched from *God's Not Dead*, so encourage your group members to pay close attention during each weekly video session. There will also be a series of questions designed to engage your group with the principles of that week's Bible study.

Also, during the sessions, encourage members to share what they have been learning from the discussion sessions and how God has been speaking to their hearts about what they've read and studied that week.

Remember that the *God's Not Dead: What Do You Believe? DVD-Based Study* should help each of your group members seek God and discover great truths from God's Word. Your small group will help members dig deeper into the topic for that week; and the video will help illustrate the concepts being studied.

Session Timing
Each weekly session is designed to be approximately ninety minutes. The length of the session will vary depending on the level of group participation and how well the discussion stays focused.

You can manage your group by encouraging everyone to participate in the discussions, but also by reminding them to keep their answers brief to allow everyone a chance to contribute. Keep the discussion focused on the topic and on the specific question the group is addressing. Small-group meetings are a great time to share conversation and build friendships, but you can arrange for snacks and social time after the group discussion is completed. If the conversation strays to other topics, gently redirect the group back to the guide's small-group study and discussion questions.

If you have less than ninety minutes available for your group, or if the discussion tends to take longer, you can carefully select which questions to cover. As you grow to know each of the group members, you'll gain a feel for which questions will most benefit your group.

Rice Broocks is the author of *God's Not Dead: Evidence for God in an Age of Uncertainty (The Evidence Behind the Movie)*. Rice is the cofounder of the Every Nation family of churches, which currently has more than one thousand churches and hundreds of campus ministries in more than sixty nations. He is also the senior minister of Bethel World Outreach Church in Nashville, Tennessee, a multiethnic, multisite church. Rice has a master's degree from Reformed Theological Seminary and a doctorate from Fuller Theological Seminary.